ORIENTAL
CARPETS
—— IN ——
MINIATURE

ORIENTAL CARPETS

— IN —

MINIATURE

CHARTED DESIGNS FOR
NEEDLEPOINT OR WHAT YOU WILL

FRANK M. COOPER

INTERWEAVE PRESS

Design, Signorella Graphic Arts
Photography, Joe Coca
Illustration, Susan Strawn
Production, Marc McCoy Owens
Computerized charts, Michael Malone Productions

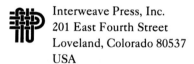 Interweave Press, Inc.
201 East Fourth Street
Loveland, Colorado 80537
USA

Library of Congress Cataloging-in-Publication Data
Cooper, Frank M., 1908–
    Oriental carpets in miniature : charted designs for needlepoint
or what you will / Frank M. Cooper.
        p.   cm.
    Includes bibliographical references and index.
    ISBN 0-934026-98-X : $16.95
    1. Canvas embroidery—Patterns.   2. Miniature fiberwork.
3. Rugs, Oriental.   I. Title
TT778.C3C665   1994
746.44'2041—dc20   94-25406
                                                    CIP

First printing:IWP—10M:994:QUE

ACKNOWLEDGEMENTS

I would like to thank Joan Knight Sherman and others at The Studio in Kansas City, Missouri, for their help in all aspects of needlepoint. I also want to thank the Toy & Miniature Museum in Kansas City for lending me two Shirvan rugs to photograph and include in this book.

Frank M. Cooper

A Shirvan Carpet

The author's hand-drawn chart for a Shirvan Carpet.

CONTENTS

INTRODUCTION

The needlepoint designs in this book have been inspired by rugs I have seen in various museums and in several books in my library. Some are inspired by antique rugs, and others by rugs of the nineteenth and twentieth centuries, but I have selected all of them because of their interesting patterns and beautiful, sometimes bold, colors.

The original rugs may have been made by nomadic weavers, by persons living in small villages, or by those living in large towns and working in carpet-weaving workshops. Regardless of when, where, and by whom they were made, the original rugs were all woven on looms. Most have pile surfaces created by hand-tied knots made of wool yarn. The two kilims (pages 76 and 114), flat-woven rugs, have no knots.

TRIBAL CARPET-WEAVING

The nomad weaver had everything needed for rug-making at hand. The loom, which was little more than a crude frame, could be made from tall, straight trees. On this frame, the weaver tightly wound a continuous strand of yarn, from top to bottom, around both the top and bottom cross beams. This vertically wound thread is called the warp. In the process of weaving, horizontal threads, called weft, pass in front of and behind alternate vertical threads. To create the rug's pile, the weaver tied yarn around two adjacent vertical warp threads. After a complete row of knots had been tied, the weaver passed a weft thread through the warp threads and, with a comb, pushed the knots and the weft thread down to the bottom of the loom. These

Nomadic weavers create colorful, richly patterned carpets on simple, portable looms, often constructed from long, straight, tree limbs, as shown here. (Photo by Paul M. Shaper ©1973.)

Oriental rugs became so popular throughout Europe that, as early as the fourteenth century, carpet-weaving workshops developed to keep up with the demand. This modern-day weaver works in a rug factory in Mashad, Iran.

(Photo by Paul M. Shaper ©1973.)

continuous weft threads, passing back and forth across the warp, help keep the knots in place and give the rug a certain amount of its body.

The yarn was made from the wool of the weaver's own sheep. The sheep were sheared by members of the family or tribe, and the wool was carded, spun into yarn, and dyed in their own small vats. Due to the vat size, only limited quantities of yarn could be dyed at one time, which sometimes resulted in a variation in the colors of the rug—just as can happen today when yarns from different dye lots are used in one piece.

The dyes were made according to "secret" formulas of each tribe, but the materials were usually the same. The madder plant was used for reds, indigo for blues, and roots of plants, bark of trees, and other natural materials for other colors. The quality of the color was affected by the water and also by the mordants used in the dyeing process.

The countryside in which the weavers lived was often dull and colorless, so the lively colors of their rugs did much to brighten their lives. The rugs were used over windows and doors, under the saddles of horses and camels, as covers for sleeping, and on the floors of the yurts. Yurts (large, portable felt structures) are a kind of tent with dirt floors, hot in the summer, cold in the winter, and dirty all the time. The rugs provide some warmth and keep down the ever-present dust. (We once drove from Kabul to Bamiyan, Afghanistan, a distance of about 150 miles. The dust was so bad that, when we reached our hotel, which was a group of slightly larger than usual yurts, and unzipped our bags, the design of the zipper was clearly outlined on the contents.)

WEAVING WORKSHOPS AND COURT RUGS

As early as the fourteenth century, Turkey developed a sea trade with Italy, and rugs are depicted in the paintings of that period, notably those by the Italian, Lorenzo Lotto, and the German, Hans Holbein. Holbein so often featured a double-medallion rug design that rugs with this feature came to be known as "Holbein Rugs." (A miniature rug, adapted from a painting by the fifteenth century painter, Hans Memling, is shown on page 31.)

As a result of trade with Italy and other European countries, the demand for rugs became so great that a "cottage industry" developed. However, even this could not keep up with the demand, so carpet-weaving workshops were set up in which many rugs could be produced at the same time. Here an overseer, referring to cartoons furnished by the workshop owner, would call out the design and color to the weaver. Many of the weavers were children, not yet in their teens, who, with their supple fingers, could tie as many as 10,000 knots in a day. All of the supplies were furnished by the workshop, and sometimes were provided to the cottage industries. No longer were the tribal designs and colors used—instead the colors and patterns were determined by fashion.

During the Safavid dynasty (1501–1734) in Persia (now Iran), the highly touted "court rugs" came into being. Their manufacture reached its peak during the reign of Shah Abbas (1589–1627). These rugs were particularly beautiful, for their designs had been produced by highly trained artists, many of whom had illustrated manuscripts and painted in miniature. These curvilinear and elaborate designs were very unlike the rectilinear, simple designs of the tribal rugs. Some of these large and beautiful rugs were sent, as gifts, to the monarchs of Europe, and hung on the walls of palaces and cathedrals, not only for decoration, but also to provide some warmth to the bare, cold stone walls.

MODERN-DAY USES FOR RUGS AND RUG MINIATURES

The inhabitants of urban areas may have used rugs for the same purposes that the nomads used theirs, but I've discovered at least one other use. While living in Meshed, Iran, in 1966–1967,

Throughout the history of Turkey, the Caucasus, and Iran, richly patterned, multicolored carpets have been woven on simple, often portable looms. These southern Persian Nomad women are from the Qashga'i tribe in Firusabad, Iran. (Photo by Paul M. Shaper ©1973.)

Finished rugs being transported for sale in the marketplace in Iran. (Photo by Paul M. Shaper ©1973.)

I was invited to the airport to meet the president of Iraq—not personally, of course, but just to be one of the crowd. With thousands of Meshedi, we lined the edge of the path that he would take to the terminal. After he landed, not once did his feet touch bare ground. Instead, he walked on Oriental rugs for a distance of several hundred feet.

I was a consultant to the Presbyterian hospitals in Iran. Our gardener acquired three pieces of property during the land reform. He sold one to get money for a pilgrimage to Mecca, the goal of all devout Muslims. On his return, he invited many of his male friends to dinner, and I was fortunate enough to be included. After I had reached his garden, like the president of Iraq, not once did my feet touch bare ground. I walked on rugs. These were not the property of the gardener, but had been rented by his friends and loaned to him for the occasion. A room-sized rug could be rented for the equivalent of 35 cents.

Just as full-sized rugs have been used in many ways, so can the miniature rugs pictured in this book be used in many ways. I have given two to the Toy & Miniature Museum in Kansas City, Missouri, to use on the floors of their dollhouses. You can also use them under lamps on tables or hang them on a wall, just as you would a picture.

I have certainly enjoyed making these needlepoint charts and rugs and hope you will get an equal amount of pleasure from them.

BEFORE YOU BEGIN

Unlike the woven, hand-knotted rugs briefly described in the Introduction, the miniature rugs shown on the following pages have been worked with needle and wool on needlepoint canvas. (You can, of course, also work them using any other type of craft that requires charted designs.)

For the rugs shown in this book, I used two different types of needlepoint stitches. The Continental Stitch (p. 15) is used to make outlines and single rows of design. The Basketweave Stitch (p. 15) is used for larger portions of the design and background.

The colors of the needlepoint rugs duplicate, as closely as possible, the colors in the original rugs I've studied. When working from photographs in books, this was difficult to achieve, because the colors shown in one illustration often differ from those in another illustration of the same rug. For example, in a picture in one book, the background of a rug was a rather dark blue. A picture of the same rug in another book showed this background as a very light, almost pastel, blue. Such are the vagaries of reproducing photographs. I've compensated by studying rugs from the same area and using their colors in the adaptation. The design and colors of the original of the rug shown on page 53 were so worn and faded that it was necessary to turn the rug over and work from the reverse side.

All of the miniature rugs shown in this book have been worked in Paternayan wool yarn on #18 canvas. In the instructions for the individual rugs, I have provided the yarn colors, with the manufacturer's identifying numbers, and the *approximate* number of 34-inch strands you'll

need. I have underlined "approximate", and this is really what I mean. You will, I believe, not run out of any of your colors. The dimensions I've given for each finished needlepoint rug are based on these materials.

For ease of handling, I use canvas that is 4 inches wider than the finished piece—2 inches on each side. For example, for a 9 × 12-inch rug, the canvas should be about 13 × 16 inches. When the stitching is completed, you'll turn the extra canvas under and fasten it to the back of the rug. You may also want to stitch the date, your initials, and the name of the rug on this turned-under portion.

Regardless of how carefully you do your stitching, the canvas will get out of shape and must be blocked. To do this, simply dampen the rug (don't soak it) and pin it to a board, with the reverse side on top, stretching the corners so they are as square as possible. While the canvas is still damp, apply a sizing material so the dried canvas will retain its shape. A solution of Rabbit-Skin Glue is very good for this and is available at most art-supply stores.

When the rug has dried, remove it from the board, turn under the extra canvas, miter the corners (sew them down if necessary), and fasten them with a glue, such as Stitch-Witchery, which is available where dry goods and notions are sold.

To hang the miniature rug on the wall as you would a picture, simply put a piece of adhesive-backed Velcro on the wall and the wool rug will stick to it. It can be easily taken down and moved to another spot.

As you're working, you may find some differences between some of the charts and the finished rugs. When I first started charting and stitching, I was so anxious to get on with the rug that I sometimes made only a portion of the chart and worked from that. I finished the charts when I decided to do this book, and so there may be some discrepancies, most of which I have noted.

The charts in this book are about half the size of my original hand-drawn ones. Before you begin one of these designs, I suggest that you enlarge the chart 200 percent at a copy machine to make it easier to read.

When starting the first strand of yarn, hold about one inch of it against the back of the canvas, and cover it with your first few stitches. When the strand is secured, clip off any excess length. To start a new strand, insert the threaded needle into loops of finished stitches on the back side of the canvas so that it emerges at the point where you wish to begin stitching.

To finish a strand, insert the threaded needle into the loops of finished stitches on the back side of the canvas; it's best to travel back in the direction from which the yarn had been worked. When you have secured about an inch of yarn, carry the needle out of the loops and cut the strand so that the tail is completely concealed. Do not secure a dark colored yarn under a row worked in light colored yarn as the darker color will show through. In general, stitch light colors first.

The needlepoint stitches that I have used in the miniature rugs throughout this book are diagonal stitches that cross the intersection of vertical and horizontal threads in the canvas. Although they are worked differently, Continental Stitch and Basketweave Stitch look the same on the front of the canvas.

CONTINENTAL STITCH

This stitch is used for outlining and for making single straight rows.

Continental stitch is always worked from right to left, across an intersection of horizontal and vertical canvas threads. Begin each new stitch in the opening to the left of the one in which you started the previous stitch. If you are working more than one row, turn the canvas upside down and work the second row from right to left again. For a third row, turn the canvas again.

If you are working a vertical or diagonal line, work the stitches from top to bottom. Turn the canvas for alternate rows so that you can work the stitches in the correct direction.

BASKETWEAVE STITCH

This sturdy stitch is used to cover the background and fill in large areas of patterning.

Basketweave stitch is made up of staggered rows of diagonal stitches. The rows are worked alternately, first down the canvas and then up. Make a stitch that crosses an intersection of horizontal and vertical threads from lower left to upper right. Skip down one hole of the canvas and make a second diagonal stitch parallel to and below the first, as shown in the drawing. Continue stitching on this diagonal for the length of the area you wish to cover. Place the first stitch of the row that will travel upward directly below the last stitch of the downward row you've just finished, as if making vertical Continental stitches. Now continue stitching on the diagonal, working from bottom to top, so that the two rows of stitches are interlocking. At the top of the work, make one stitch to the left of the completed row so that you can begin another downward row.

CONTINENTAL STITCH

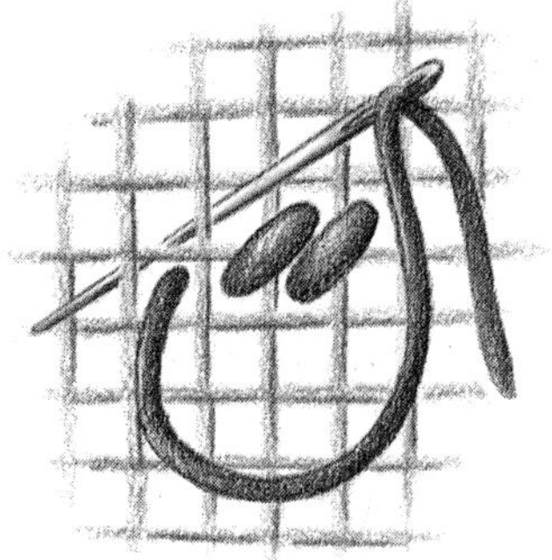

Working right to left, start each stitch in the opening to the left of the previous one.

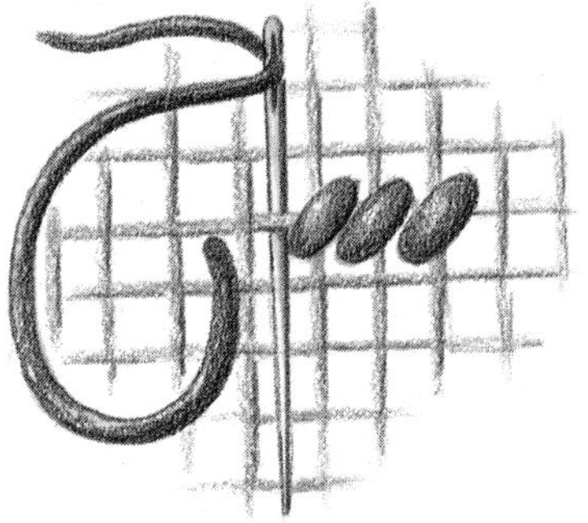

Start the second row by inserting the needle into the row below and turning your work 180 degrees.

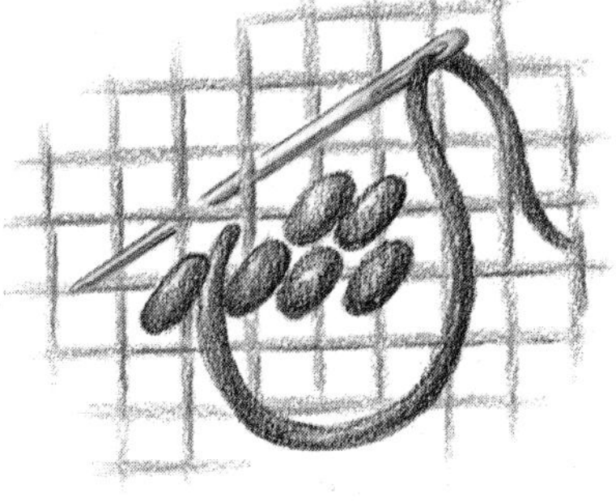

Continue working right to left above the first row.

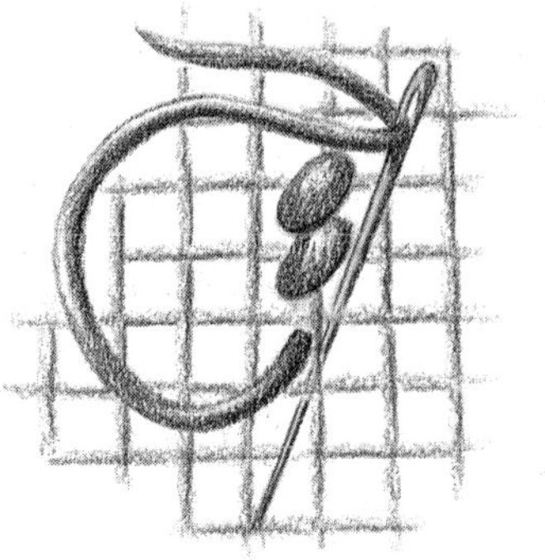

Work vertical stitches top to bottom.

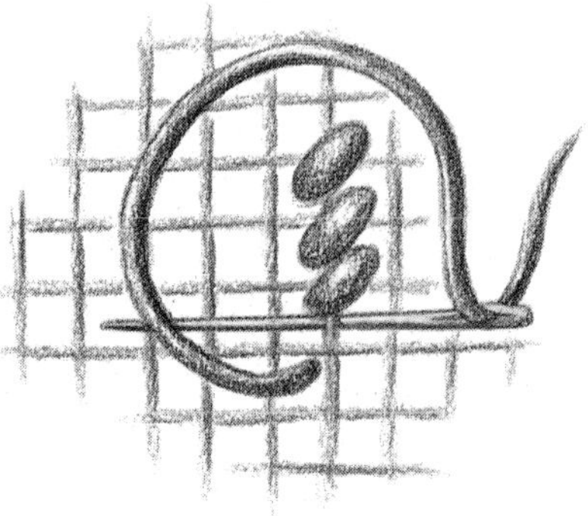

Start the second row by inserting the needle into the row to the left and turning your work 180 degrees.

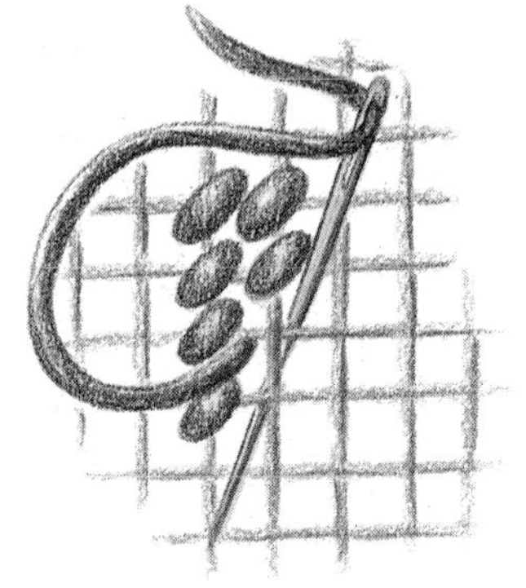

Continue working top to bottom.

BASKETWEAVE STITCH

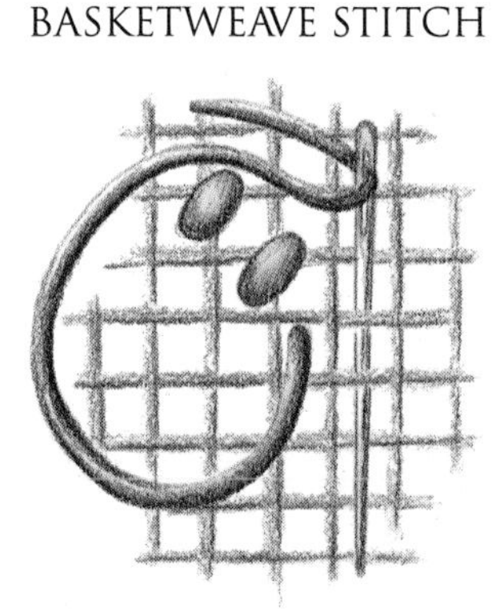

Work the first row diagonally from top to bottom.

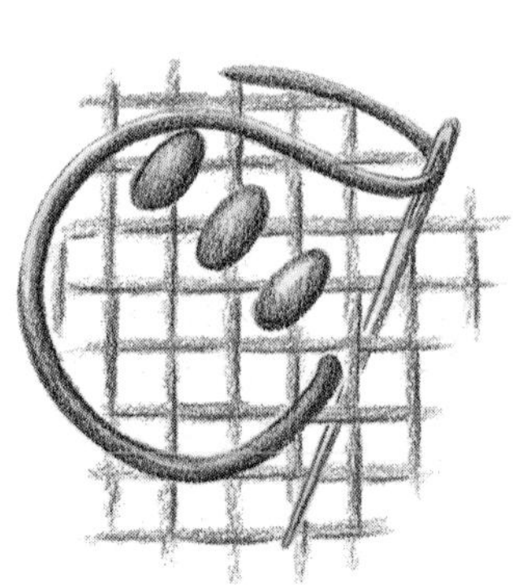

Start the second row by inserting the needle in the space directly below the last stitch.

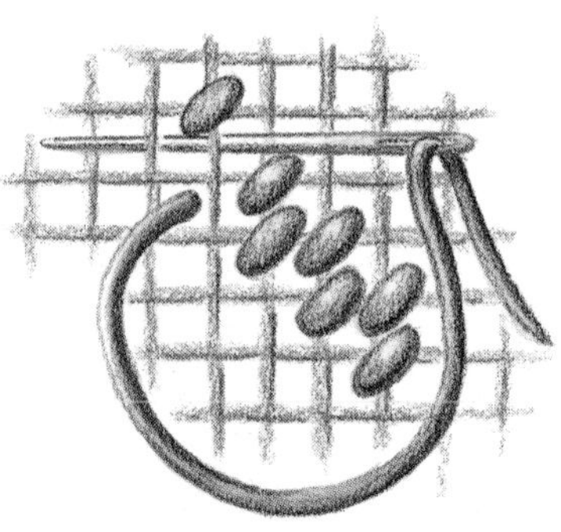

Work the next row diagonally from bottom to top.

Here, the same motif has been worked on four different gauges of canvas.

TURKISH RUGS

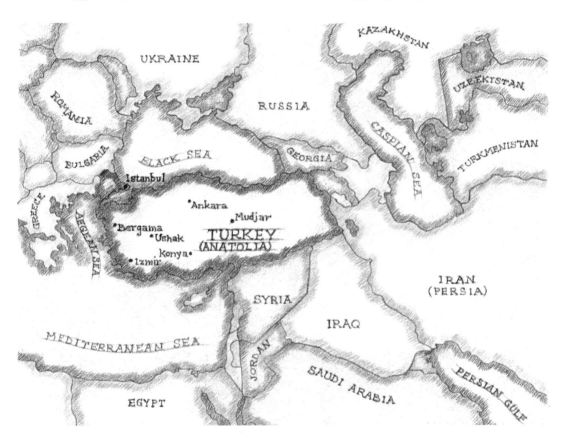

KONYA

When the Seljuks of Turkestan overran the Near East in the eleventh century, they captured the city of Konya. It was located in the midst of a well-watered oasis on a much traveled east-west highway, and the conquerers realized its importance. They established one of their Sultanates here, which became known for its opulence and culture. Marco Polo visited Konya at the end of the thirteenth century and noted that fine and beautiful carpets were produced there. Only a few remnants have survived, however, and they are now in the collection of the Museum of Turkish and Islamic Art in Istanbul.

Through the years, devout Muslims have given their prized rugs to the mosques, and as a result, there were often several layers of rugs on the mosque floors. In recent years, less devout persons began removing and disposing of these rugs. To preserve and display them, the Vakiflar Hali Muzesi in Istanbul has collected and saved these prizes.

I photographed this first rug in the museum. The labels were written in Turkish, which I cannot read, and there was no one to translate for me. So I do not know the date it was woven and, until recently when it was identified as a Konya, I did not know its place of origin.

124 × 221 stitches
#18 canvas (18 per 2.5 cm)
7 × 12¼ inches (17.9 × 31.4 cm)

Colors	Dark Blue	Light Blue	Beige	Red	Green	Brown
Yarn #	500	503	443	870	641	440
Strands	17	1	21	30	8	7
Symbol	■	◪	☐	⊡	⊠	◨

ANATOLIAN

This dragon-and-phoenix design is adapted from an Anatolian rug that can be dated, with some accuracy, as fifteenth century. A very similar design is depicted in a fresco by Domenico di Bartolo, entitled "The Wedding of the Foundlings", dated between 1440 and 1444.

Wilhelm von Bode, a German scholar, found this rug in Italy and acquired it in 1886. It now hangs in a Berlin museum. The yellow background, rarely found in such profusion in Turkish rugs, seems to signify Chinese influence, as does the dragon-and-phoenix design, which may be a geometrical rendering of an older Chinese motif. According to Wilhelm von Bode, it may have had four or six panels of the same design.

The Berlin Rug, as it is known, measures 35 × 68 inches. It does not have a border on the right, but I have included one in my adaptation.

I also made a change after I drew the design for this rug. The chart shows that blue yarn is used for the narrow stripes on either side of the 'S' design in the main border. This is not correct. I substituted brown in place of blue in the stripes.

139 × 247 stitches
#18 canvas (18 per 2.5 cm)
$7^5/_8 \times 13^3/_4$ inches (19.6 × 35.3 cm)

Colors	Red	Cream	Brown	Blue	Yellow
Yarn #	861	745	420	500	733
Strands	30	14	20	20	36
Symbol	⊡	◪	⊠	■	☐

MUDJAR

The spelling of the name of the town from which this rug came varies depending on the book you are reading or the map you are studying: Mujur, Mudjur, Mudjar—take your choice. I adapted this design from an illustration in the book *Oriental Carpets* by Ulrich Schurmann, and so I really should spell it his way, which is Mujur, but so many books and maps use the spelling Mudjar that I have decided to go with the majority.

The colors in Mudjar rugs are more varied than in others of Anatolian origin. In this design, you find mauve, pink, blue, green, and shades of yellow, which you may not find combined in other rugs from this area.

The series of prayer arches depicted in this rug is very rare to find. The original rug dates from the first part of the nineteenth century, and is in a private collection. The original rug, from which this design was adapted, measures $42\frac{1}{4} \times 59\frac{3}{4}$ inches.

159 × 239 stitches
#18 canvas (18 per 2.5 cm)
$8\frac{7}{8} \times 13\frac{1}{4}$ inches (22.7 × 34 cm)

Colors	Rose (Red)	Gold	Mauve	Ivory	Blue	Brown	Green	Beige
Yarn #	931	444	312	445	512	470	610	752
Strands	31	13	8	32	9	40	2	20
Symbol	⊡	⦿	☒	☐	⊠	■	⊙	◪

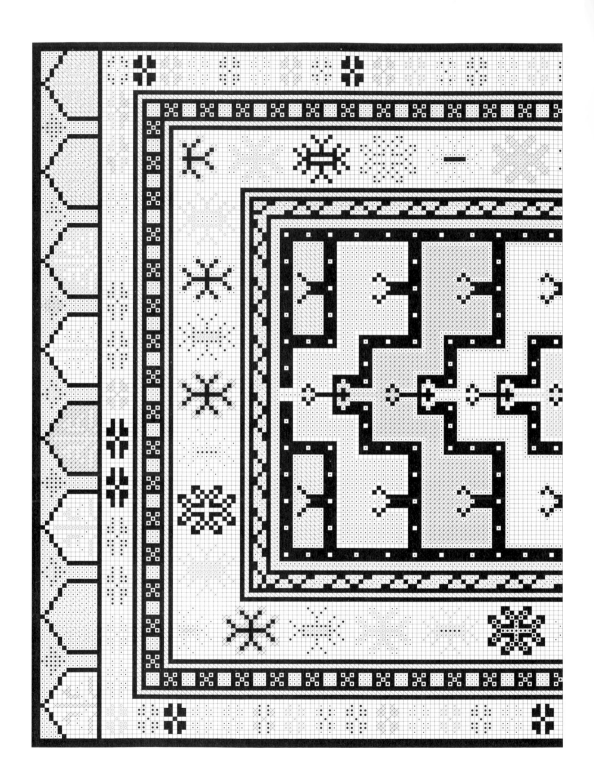

MEMLING BERGAMA

In the western part of Turkey, almost on the Aegean Sea, there is a small city called Bergamo (with an *o*) by some writers and Bergama (with an *a*) by others. The *Rand McNally World Atlas* places Bergamo in Italy and Bergama in Turkey. Because Turkish rugs are the subject here, to avoid confusion, I'll use the latter spelling.

The rug from which I've adapted this design is shown in a painting by Hans Memling, a fifteenth-century Flemish painter. The painting is now in the collection of the Baron Thyssen-Bornemisza and has been exhibited in this country. When the baron was in Kansas City and was shown this miniature, he wryly remarked that a royalty possibly would have to be paid—to Mr. Memling.

There is no assurance that this is a Bergama rug, but it meets the description given in several books, and rugs from this area were being exported to Europe as early as the fourteenth century. Because the rug appears in a Memling painting, it is, perhaps, safer to call it a Memling Bergama.

The two shades of red in this rug are so nearly the same that you may decide to use only one, which will make very little difference in the appearance of the finished rug.

155 × 161 stitches
#18 canvas (18 per 2.5 cm)
8⅝ × 9 inches (22.1 × 23.1 cm)

Colors	Dark Blue	Ivory	Red	Green	Gold	Dark Green	Dark Red
Yarn #	500	756	950	643	751	641	930
Strands	18	18	18	3	18	9	17
Symbol	■	□	⊙	⊠	◪	☒	▫

BERGAMA

The Turkish city of Bergama has been possessed by Romans, Persians, Greeks, and many others. Although nearly destroyed during the Turkish Wars, today it is a city of almost 20,000 people.

The rugs made in Bergama are usually almost square, with one or two medallions occupying the center field. These medallions are sometimes defined very clearly by surrounding lines of white or ivory, and small bits of green and yellow add interest to the borders. Although the reason is not known, the bold designs of these rugs are more like the designs of Caucasian rugs than like those of other Turkish rugs.

If interrupted by a visitor, the weaver of a Bergama rug, wanting to ward off the "evil eye", will often ask for a small patch of the visitor's garment and will sew this onto the rug. With additional interruptions, buttons or tassels may be attached to the rug.

The inspiration for this rug dates from about 1800 and is illustrated in *Oriental Carpets* by Ulrich Schurmann. The original measures 56 × 72 inches. The border in this miniature is filled with archaic S-forms.

143 × 184 stitches
#18 canvas (18 per 2.5 cm)
8 × 10¼ inches (20.5 × 26.3 cm).

Colors	Blue	Gold	Ivory	Red	Green	Brown or Black
Yarn #	501	752	261	850	643	450 or 220
Strands	18	6	8	45	10	15
Symbol	■	◨	☐	⊡	⊠	⊙

USHAK 1

I hesitate to put a date on the beautiful and unusual Ushak rug from which I adapted this miniature. The book *Oriental Carpets* lists it as seventeenth century. Wilhelm von Bode, for a number of reasons, says it should be placed ahead of all other Ushak prayer rugs, some of which are known to be sixteenth century. Whatever its age, it is an outstanding design and the colors are exceptional. This rug is now in the Islamic Museum in Berlin.

The design in the outer border is charted red and gold, but when I made the piece I changed it to red and white.

156 × 229 stitches
#18 canvas (18 per 2.5 cm)
8⅝ × 12¾ inches (22.1 × 32.7 cm)

Colors	Red	Dark Red	Dark Blue	Light Blue	Gray	White	Purple	Gold
Yarn #	861	870	221	212	200	445	921	733
Strands	41	9	60	16	6	8	4	4
Symbol	●	◹	▨	⊠	◺	□	◤	◉

USHAK 2

A white Ushak carpet was my inspiration for the design of this needlepoint rug. The original is in the McMullan Collection at the Metropolitan Museum of Art in New York City. It could, however, just as well have been adapted from a carpet illustrated in *Oriental Carpets*, described as being 94 × 193 inches and dating somewhere from the sixteenth to seventeenth centuries. The two rugs are almost identical in design, and the colors are very much the same.

This carpet is called the "Bird Rug." The birds, together with a floral motif, fill the entire light-colored field. Some writers say that the bird is actually a stylized flower. Nathaniel Harris, in his book, *Rugs & Carpets of the Orient*, claims that the motif resembles a bird because the geometric shape has been so ornamented that it seems a beak, tail, and wing have been formed.

This rug and the Ushak on p. 47 are among several from this area having white or light-colored fields. The usual Anatolian rug of this period makes use of brilliant reds and blues in the field.

158 × 234 stitches
#18 canvas (18 per 2.5 cm)
8³⁄₄ × 13 inches (22.4 × 33.3 cm)

Colors	Red	Green	Blue	Gold	Ivory
Yarn #	940	520	500	752	445
Strands	26	16	4	19	60
Symbol	⊙	⊠	■	◿	☐

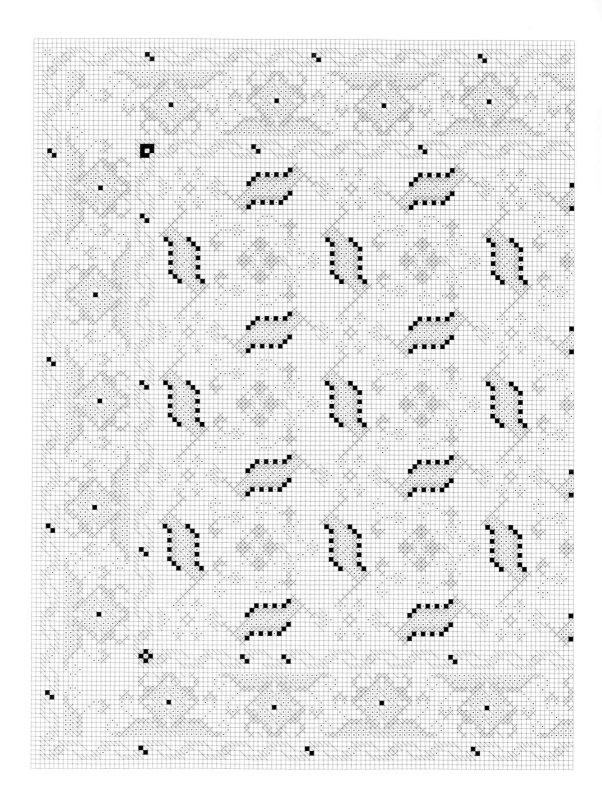

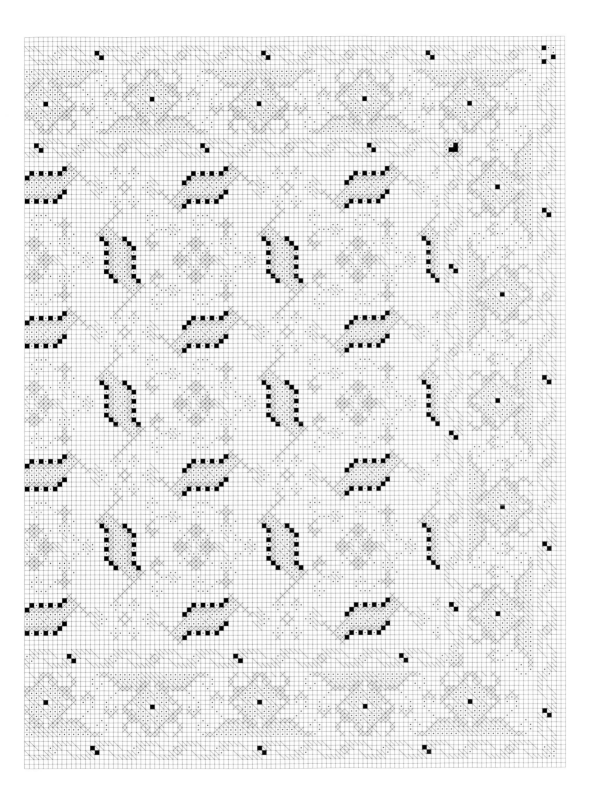

USHAK 3

The design for this miniature was adapted from a large carpet woven especially for the reception hall of the Harem in the Topaki Sarayi Muzesi in Istanbul, Turkey. In his letter to me of August, 1980, A. S. Duruçay, director of the museum, identified the carpet as a copy of an older rug. He did not mention the date of the original carpet, although he implied that it might be seventeenth century. The copy was made in Kayseri about 1968–1969.

There are several theories as to the origin of the design. Some say it evolved from the Three Pearls of Wisdom of Buddhism; others say that it was the insignia of the Mongolian conqueror, Timur; others simply call it a thunder and lightning pattern. Regardless of its origin, we know that this design found its way across Central Asia and was popular in Turkey in the fifteenth century. It was one of the most desired designs of the Ottoman period and can be found on fabrics, ceramics, and even on the tiles decorating some of the mosques.

As you look through books showing Oriental rugs, you will probably see a design similar to this one, in which there will be two wavy lines, one right above the other. I tried to put in both wavy lines, but the design didn't look right to me, so I left one out.

174 × 228 stitches
#18 canvas (18 per 2.5 cm)
9⅝ × 12⅝ inches (24.7 × 32.4 cm)

Colors	Dark Blue	Light Blue	Red	Ivory	Purple	Gold
Yarn #	512	523	873	263	310	742
Strands	24	14	28	65	2	2
Symbol	■	⊠	⊡	☐	◪	◩

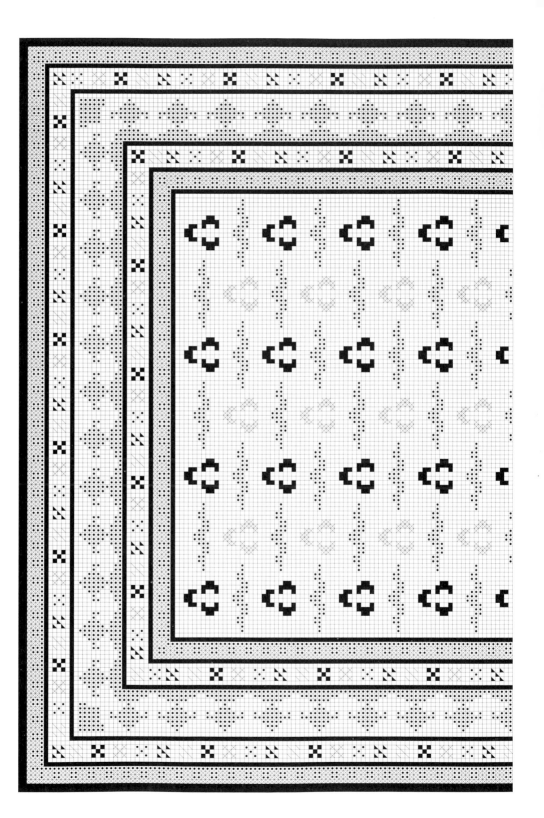

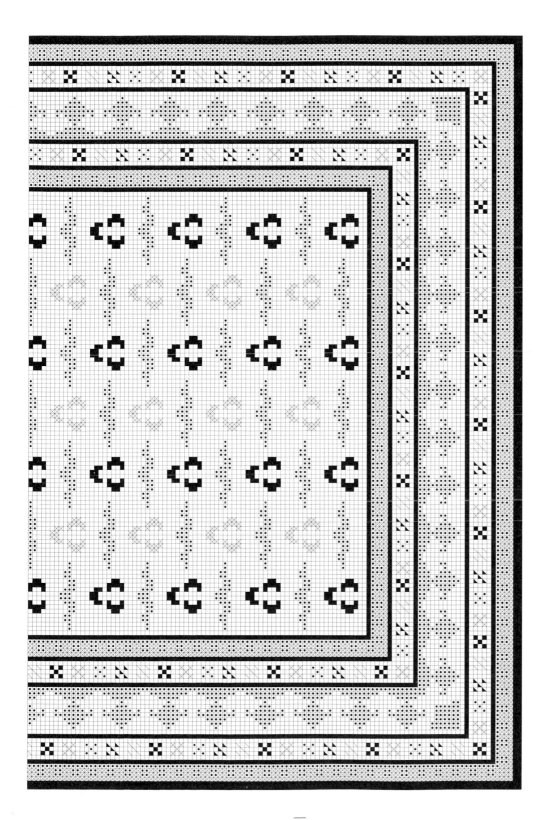

CAUCASIAN RUGS

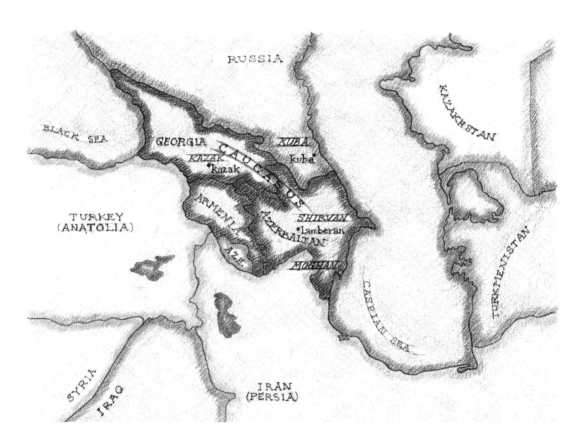

KAZAK 1

The Kazak rug from which I adapted this design is in The Nelson-Atkins Museum of Art, Kansas City, Missouri. The bright colors and bold designs are typical of rugs from this area. In the center of each of the two medallions, which almost cover the entire field, is a gold square containing what appears to be a swastika. This, in turn, is surrounded by eight cloud bands, and rugs with this design are sometimes called "cloud band" Kazaks. Some writers call these bands "dragons."

Unfortunately, the original rug is now so badly worn that in some spots you see nothing but warp and weft threads. Although the design is still fairly well defined, I had to reverse the rug and look at it from the back side to see the true colors. The original rug is $55\frac{1}{2} \times 72\frac{1}{2}$ inches.

The wide, light-colored border, with its stylized "eagle beaks" or "eagle heads" design is very much like the Shirvan rug shown on p. 81. This popular design is found in many rugs from this area. The reciprocal trefoil design found in the two narrow borders is also much used in these rugs.

177 × 294 stitches
#18 canvas (18 per 2.5 cm)
$9\frac{1}{2} \times 16\frac{1}{2}$ inches (24.4 × 42.3 cm)

Colors	Red	Blue	Gold	Green	Ivory	Brown	Black
Yarn #	951	501	742	610	445	440	420
Strands	50	16	12	14	40	10	38
Symbol	●	X	◹	⊠	☐	O	■

KAZAK 2

This unusual needlepoint design was inspired by a lively rug in the McMullan Collection in the Metropolitan Museum of Art in New York City. There is also one very similar to it in the Ballard Collection in the City Art Museum in St. Louis, Missouri.

This rug is unmistakably a Kazak, recognizable by its widely spaced decoration on a plain-colored field, which creates an impression of largeness. As are the other Kazaks shown in this book, this rug is a good example of the startling, unexpected, and extremely interesting color contrasts employed by these weavers. The original rug is 71 × 96 inches.

The wide white border is filled with highly stylized Kufic script, separated by Mystic knots, which are symbolic of God. The illiterate could gain merit just by looking at the script, which contains the Prophet's sacred words.

The yarn count given here is very generous, and you may end up with a little more than you really need. You won't run out—that's for sure.

159 × 213 stitches
#18 canvas (18 per 2.5 cm)
9 × 12 inches (23.1 × 30.8 cm)

Colors	Blue	Ivory	Red	Green	Gold
Yarn #	500	445	950	610	752
Strands	60	30	50	10	24
Symbol	■	□	⊙	⊠	◿

KAZAK 3

The carpets of the Caucasian people reflect tribal differences, but although the designs vary from one place to another, there are similarities that distinguish them from all other rugs. This is especially true of the rugs from the Kazak area. The large, well-outlined designs are usually geometric shapes, and the colors are bright with very little shading. The designs seem to float on the background with no connecting lines holding them together.

This design is adapted from a picture on the dust cover of Nathaniel Harris's book, *Rugs and Carpets of the Orient*. The size of the original rug is unknown to me. This red-and-green prayer rug is particularly interesting because of the very complex shape within the larger green medallion, set off by the brown-and-white border with its multitude of small figures. At first glance, all the little figures seem to be the same size, but they measure differently on each of the four sides. At the center of the right side, one of the small brown figures seems to have two "heads" and the next one has none. This bit of whimsy would not occur in a machine-made rug, but adds vitality and interest in a hand-made rug like this one.

As the devout Moslem kneels upon his prayer rug five times each day to pray, he intones this prayer:

In the name of God, the Compassionate, the Merciful
Praise be to God, Lord of the Worlds!
The compassionate, the merciful!
King on the day of reckoning!
Thee only do we worship, and to Thee do we cry for help.
Guide Thou us on the straight path,
The path of those to whom Thou hast been gracious;
With whom Thou art not angry, and who do not go astray.

154 × 201 stitches
#18 canvas (18 per 2.5 cm)
8½ × 11½ inches (21.8 × 29.5 cm)

Colors	Ivory	Red	Green	Brown	Gold	Dark Green
Yarn #	445	951	521	420	752	520
Strands	33	44	14	15	4	36
Symbol	☐	⊡	⊠	O	◹	■

KAZAK 4

This is the fourth and last of the Kazak rugs. With its large, outlined, free-floating figures, by now you would probably recognize it without being told its name.

The colors are bright and rich, with a liberal amount of green. The large center figure is perfectly balanced by smaller figures on all sides. The wide primary border contains crablike figures, as well as what seems to be a serrated and stylized leaf pattern. The guard stripes, which separate the main border from the field and other borders, are composed of the ubiquitous trefoil pattern and dotted lines.

This design is adapted from the end papers of Nathaniel Harris's book, *Rugs and Carpets of the Orient*. In the original rug and on the chart, the top and bottom borders carry the same pattern, which is slightly different from that of the side borders. When I made the miniature, however, I inadvertently carried the side-border design across the bottom border.

161 × 273 stitches
#18 canvas (18 per 2.5 cm)
9 × 15 inches (23.1 × 38.5 cm)

Colors	Orange (Red)	Brown	Green	Ivory	Gold
Yarn #	861	420	642	444	414
Strands	43	33	27	18	10
Symbol	☐	■	⊠	⊡	◻

CAUCASIAN 1

This rug is in the McMullan Collection in the Metropolitan Museum of Art, New York, where it is identified simply as Caucasian. Someone further classified it as a Moghan rug, and after seeing a very similar design in the Ian Bennett book, *Rugs & Carpets of the World,* I am sure this designation is correct.

The Moghan area is in southern Azerbaijan, right on the Iranian border. The area is a veritable melting pot of many cultures and religions. For hundreds of years, before it became a part of Russia, it was a battleground for Arabs, Mongols, Turks, Persians, and Russians, all striving to make the region theirs. Naturally, these various cultures left their imprints on the inhabitants of the area, which is reflected in the rugs of the region.

The design of the woven rug is very similar to some seen in early European paintings and in Timurid miniatures of the late 14th century. The design is very adaptable, and the size of the rug can be changed simply by adding or subtracting "tiles".

In this rug, you can see a contemporary example of abrash, the natural variations that occur in different dye lots. I ran out of red yarn while vacationing in France and, with my very limited knowledge of the French language, I had a bad time trying to match the yarn. I finally found some a shade darker and was happy to get it.

At first glance, this rug seems to have little color in it other than the red, dark blue, white, and some green in the triangles and border. Looking more closely, however, you will find a lighter shade of blue as well as gold. The stars within the octagons are the same design, but the colors vary. The small squares in the borders are placed very randomly, so do these any way you want.

171 × 211 stitches
#18 canvas (18 per 2.5 cm)
$9^1/_2 × 11^3/_4$ inches (24.4 × 30.1 cm)

Colors	Dark Blue	Lighter Blue	Ivory	Red	Green	Gold
Yarn #	570	500	465	840	610	752
Strands	28	20	25	48	10	12
Symbol	■	⊠	□	●	☒	◪

KUBA

Caucasian rugs were woven in the mountainous area between the Caspian Sea on the east and the Black Sea on the west. Over the course of time, this area has been occupied by many different peoples—Turks, Persians, Armenians, and Turkomen tribes from Central Asia. Some of these peoples have remained, and the area is now one of many tribes and tongues.

The rug patterns, varied as they may be, are generally geometric. Any curvilinear designs, resulting from the influence of other areas, have been reduced to severe straight lines. The predominant colors are red, blue, yellow, green, ivory, and occasionally brown. Star motifs form a large part of the rug decoration. Sometimes the weavers use flowers, animals, or human being motifs, but they have been rendered so geometrically that they are hard to identify.

One of their most pleasing patterns is this Kuba rug with five reddish Lesghi stars named for the Lesghian tribes with whom the design originated. These stars, with their brown centers, are placed on a dark blue, almost black, background. The field is further ornamented with squares containing different designs. The light brown main border, with its characteristic S-shaped design, is centered between two narrow borders with identically shaped rosettes.

The inspiration for this design came from a rug illustrated in *Oriental Rugs in Color* by Preben Liebetrau. The original measures 56 × 99 inches. According to Liebetrau, the quality of these Kuba rugs is among the highest in the Caucasus. They are rugs for the connoisseur.

131 × 256 stitches
#18 canvas (18 per 2.5 cm)
6¾ × 14 inches (17.3 × 35.9 cm)

Colors	Dark Blue	Dark Brown	Light Brown	Gold	Ivory	Red
Yarn #	570	430	472	742	262	931
Strands	14	16	24	6	7	40
Symbol	■	⊠	☐	◪	⊡	⊙

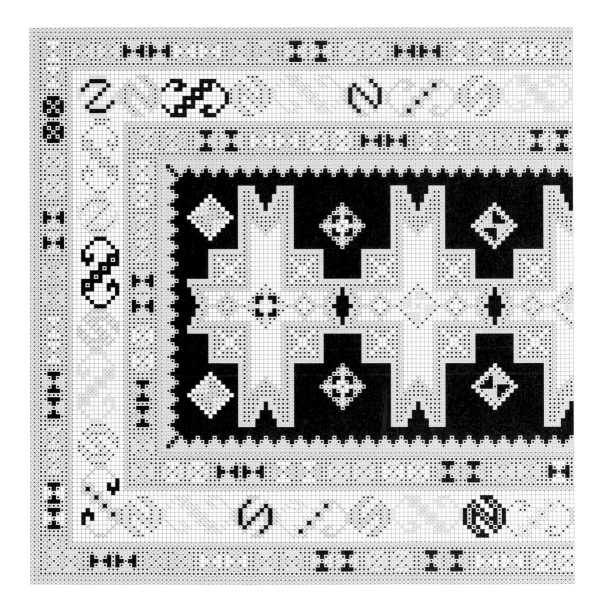

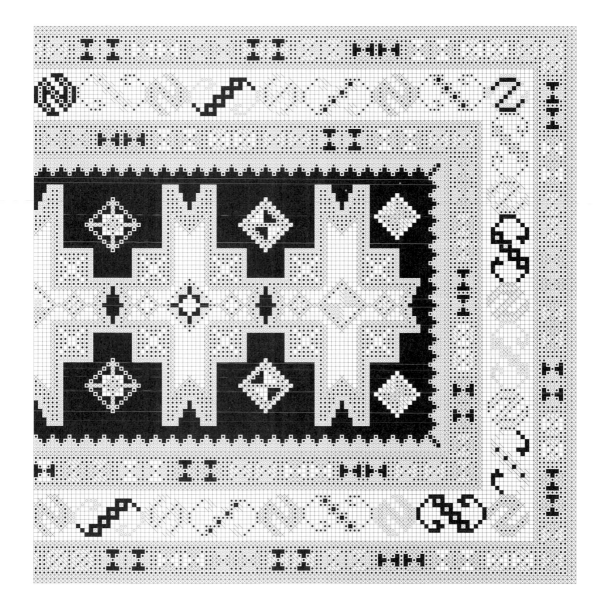

CAUCASIAN 2

In Caucasian homes, humble though they might be, pile carpets were used on the floors for warmth. Flat-woven rugs called kilims, of which this is one, were used when a more flexible material was needed. Kilims were also made into bags for storing food, household utensils, clothing, etc. Nomads also used them to make saddle bags and horse, donkey, and camel trappings.

The flat-woven carpet from which this design has been adapted dates from the eighteenth century and is illustrated in Liatif Kerimov's book, *Rugs and Carpets from the Caucasus*. The rug came from the village of Lamberan in Azerbaijan and is now in the Mustafayev Art Museum in Baku.

The colors of the Azerbaijan rugs are much more restrained than those of the nearby Kazak rugs, which have such brilliant and contrasting colors. The decorative figures in the rug may reflect the everyday environment of the weaver, which would lead us to believe that this particular kilim might have been woven by a person from a nomadic tribe.

Note how the dark brown of the main border is carried across the center portion of the rug. Only the lower half of the rug was illustrated in the book. I assumed that the top was very much the same as the bottom, and made my design accordingly.

The camels in this caravan are much more colorful than they are in real life. If camels were really these colors, the caravans would have been even more interesting than they actually were.

216 × 194 stitches
#18 canvas (18 per 2.5 cm)
12 × 10¾ inches (30.8 × 27.6 cm)

Colors	Red	Gray	Blue	Dark Brown	Light Brown	Ivory	Camel	Dark Camel
Yarn #	871	464	513	450	472	445	443	441
Strands	31	5	6	58	9	9	4	3
Symbol	⊙	☒	⊠	■	◹	☐	◣	⊠

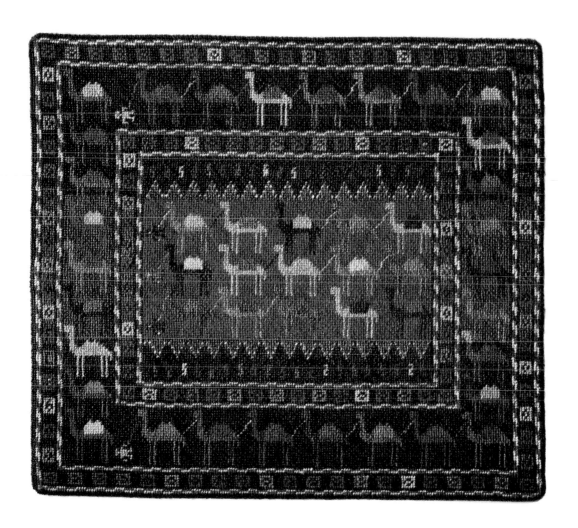

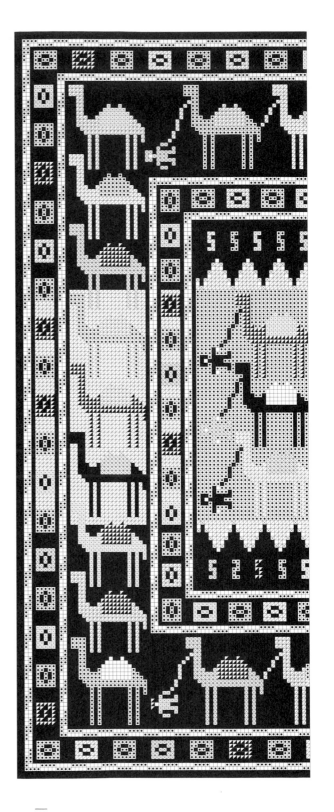

SHIRVAN 1

This rug is of particular interest because of the different shades of color in the main border. In these "eagle-head" or "eagle-beak" designs, there are three shades of red (pink) and three shades of blue-green, in addition to pale yellow, an ivory background, and dark blue outlines.

The "eagle-head" border is very similar to the main border of a Kazak rug in the collection of the Nelson-Atkins Museum of Art in Kansas City, Missouri. However, in this Shirvan rug, the colors in the main border are much more subtle, due to the shading from dark to light.

It is not surprising to find these birdlike figures on rugs from many different areas. Even though tribes tend to stay in their own areas and guard their unique rug designs, there is a certain amount of communication between tribes, and attractive designs have a tendency to spread. As you can see on the map on p. 51, the Shirvan and Kazak areas are not too far apart.

The rug that inspired this design is shown in *Oriental Carpets* by Ulrich Schurmann. It dates from the early nineteenth century, and is now in a private collection in Paris. The original rug measures 35 × 52¼ inches.

163 × 265 stitches
#18 canvas (18 per 2.5 cm)
9 × 14¾ inches (23.1 × 37.8 cm)

Colors	Dark Red	Medium Red	Light Red	Navy Blue	Dark Blue-Green	Medium Blue-Green	Light Blue-Green	White	Off-white
Yarn #	870	930	931	500	521	522	523	445	444
Strands	21	24	2	48	9	14	2	36	8
Symbol	⊙	◪	◪	■	⊠	⊠(X)	◢	☐	◿

SHIRVAN 2

This Shirvan rug is in the collection of James Forbes of San Francisco. I photographed the rug and developed a miniature design from it, which I gave to the Forbeses. I also made a second rug, which, together with the Shirvan on p. 81, I donated to the Toy & Miniature Museum, Kansas City, Missouri. They are both now on display in one of the museum's dollhouses.

The colors in this Shirvan rug and the preceding one are very much the same. Each has a dark-blue background and a wide primary border with a narrower secondary border on each side. These narrow borders are separated from the main cream-colored border by thin stripes of white or white and red.

The serrated-leaf-and-wine-glass pattern is one that you may find in Dagestan or Kabistan rugs, but is used so frequently in Shirvan rugs that it is almost typical of this area. It may have originated in Armenia, as it is similarly drawn in rugs from that area dating from about A.D. 1500. The pattern scarcely varies from time to time and place to place, except in the number of serrations in the leaf and the shape of the cup.

Even though I have made two of these rugs, I neglected to keep a record of the amount of yarn used for each color. As a result, the amounts given here are only estimates.

163 × 209 stitches
#18 canvas (18 per 2.5 cm)
9 × 11⅝ inches (23.1 × 29.8 cm)

Colors	Dark Blue	Light Blue	Red	Gold	Gray	White
Yarn #	510	512	930	742	464	445
Strands	32	13	26	15	6	28
Symbol	■	⊠	⊡	⊘	⊡	☐

SHIRVAN 3

The cottage industry has played an important role in rug weaving in Turkey, Persia (now Iran), and the Caucasus. In the seventeenth and eighteenth centuries, many of the rugs exported to Europe from western Turkey had been produced by cottage industries. Some were made under contract, with the contractor sometimes furnishing all the materials needed for making the rugs, even the looms.

The contract system was introduced into the Caucasus by the Persians in the latter part of the nineteenth century. The Persians brought with them some of the designs from the elegant court rugs. These complicated designs, however, were much too intricate for the cottage weavers. So they changed the curves into straight lines and angles and changed the sophisticated colors of the Persian rugs to the primary colors, with which the weaver were more familiar: red, blue, and yellow.

The design for this rug, which dates from the nineteenth century, was adapted from an illustration in Jon Thompson's book, *Oriental Carpets, from the Tents, Cottages, and Workshops of Asia.* The rug is described as a product of the cottage industry in Shirvan, a district in the southern part of the Caucasus. The original rug measures 36 × 48 inches.

The small spots in the diagonal stripes are shown on the chart as being three rows wide with three stitches in each row. When I started making the rug, I found that three rows with three stitches was too much, so I changed it to two rows with three stitches in each row. On the top of the rug, the seventh diagonal stripe from the left is charted as rust. When stitching the rug, I changed it to yellow.

171 × 227 stitches
#18 canvas (18 per 2.5 cm)
$9^5/_8 \times 12^3/_4$ inches (24.7 × 32.7 cm)

Colors	Dark Blue	Medium Blue	Light Blue	Red	Green	White	Beige	Rust	Yellow
Yarn #	570	500	512	930	532	262	404	871	733
Strands	47	5	2	54	19	26	15	6	2
Symbol	■	◪	⊞	⊡	⊠	□	◹	⊙	◺

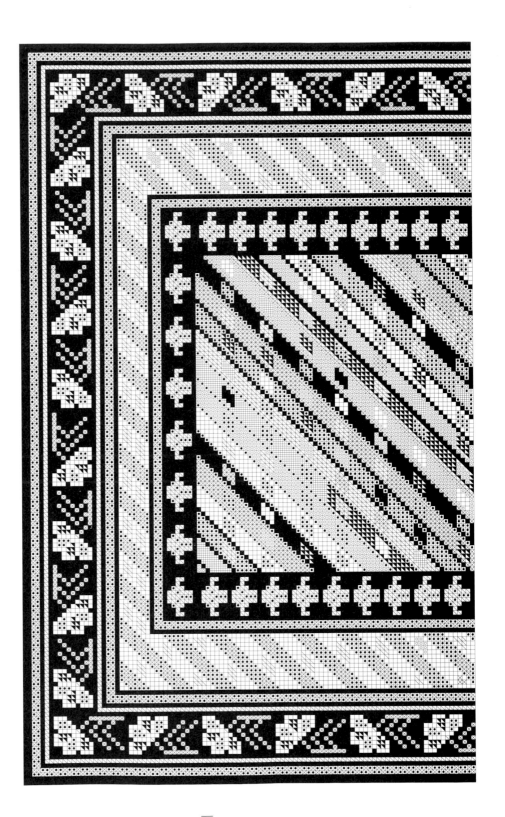

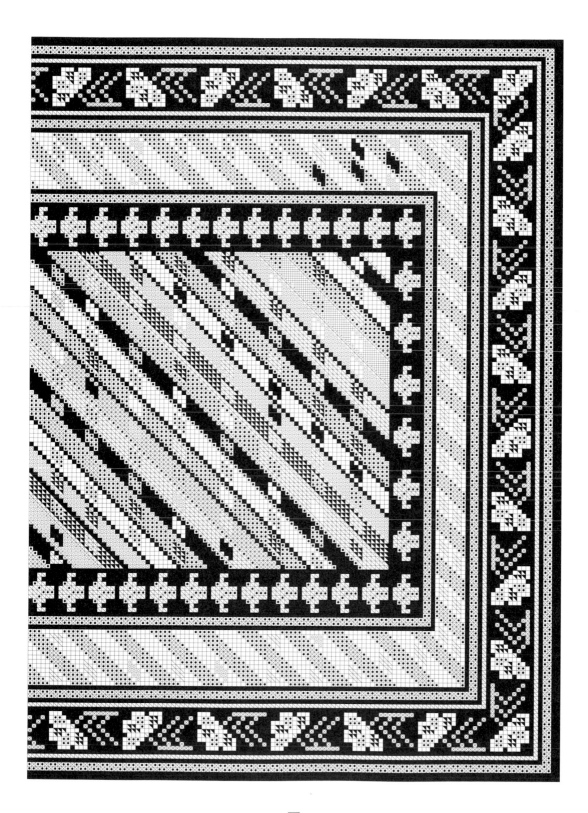

PERSIAN RUGS

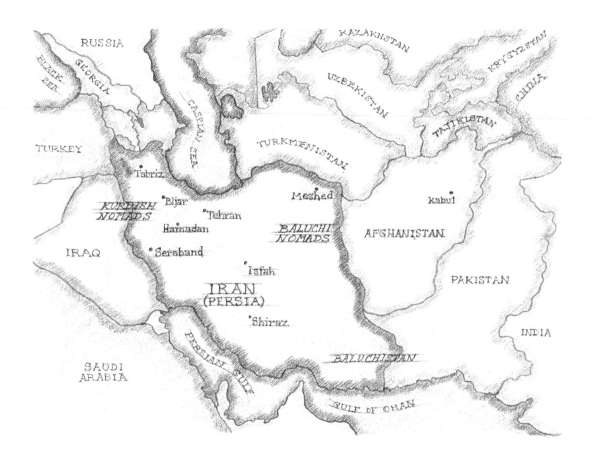

BALUCHI 1

Subdued colors are characteristic of Baluchi rugs. I found the original inspiration for this design in the collection of the Nelson-Atkins Museum of Art, Kansas City, Missouri, and was given permission to photograph it there.

Some writers say that Baluchi rugs are woven in Baluchistan, which is partly in southern Iran and partly in Pakistan. The eminent authority, Cecil Edwards, says these rugs are woven by the Baluchi tribes of northern Iran, about 100 miles south of Meshed. These tribes were brought from Baluchistan by Nadir Shah in the eighteenth century and today make up the core of the Baluchi population of the province.

The rug patterns of these tribes have remained relatively unique, for these tribes live in a very desolate area that is cut off from neighbors by deserts and mountain ridges.

When I was developing the design for this rug, I think I started in the center and worked my way out from there. I put in the small design (5 stitches), then worked the background, and then moved on to the next diagonal stripe.

159 × 229 stitches
#18 canvas (18 per 2.5 cm)
8¾ × 12¾ inches (22.4 × 32.7 cm)

Colors	White	Dark Red	Light Red	Blue-Green	Dark Brown	Medium Brown	Light Brown
Yarn #	445	870	871	520	420	450	452
Strands	18	6	36	25	10	30	10
Symbol	☐	O	•	■	◹	◪	⊠

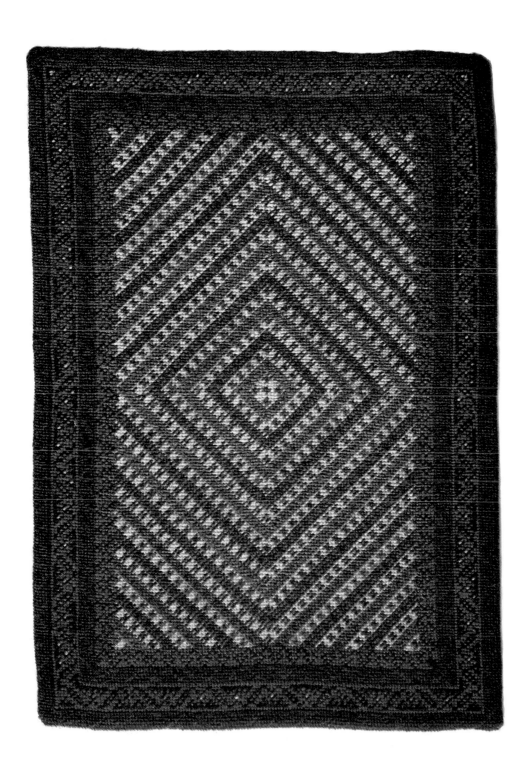

BALUCHI 2

Characteristically, the colors in this Baluchi rug are quiet and subdued. On either side of the *mihrab*, that portion of the design that is pointed toward the sacred city of Mecca during prayers, are the representation of hands. Here, the faithful place their hands as they kneel in prayer and touch their foreheads to a small tablet placed at the apex of the *mihrab*. This tablet is sometimes made of earth from Mecca.

The devoted say prayers five times each day—at sunrise, midday, four hours after midday, sunset, and about one hour later.

The woven rugs of the Baluchi tribes from northern Khorasan are superior to those woven in the south. Khorasan province is in northeastern Iran. According to Preben Liebetrau, from whose book this design was adapted, this rug came from northeast Iran, so, presumably, is one of those of better quality.

This small rug was probably made on a portable horizontal loom, which was capable of being rolled up and carried to the next campground. The original rug is 38 × 72 inches.

145 × 244 stitches
#18 canvas (18 per 2.5 cm)
8 × 13½ inches (20.5 × 34.6 cm)

Colors	Blue	Red	Ivory	Brown	Gold
Yarn #	500	930	645	441	741
Strands	40	40	14	20	4
Symbol	■	⊙	□	⊡	⧄

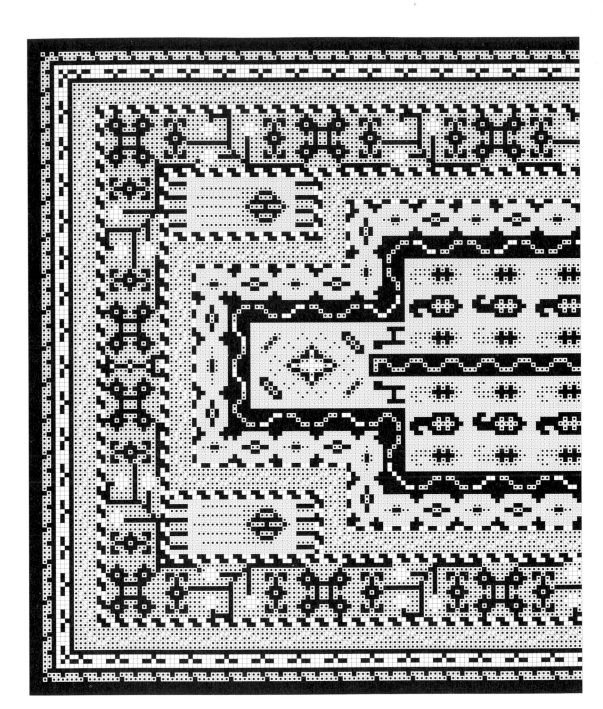

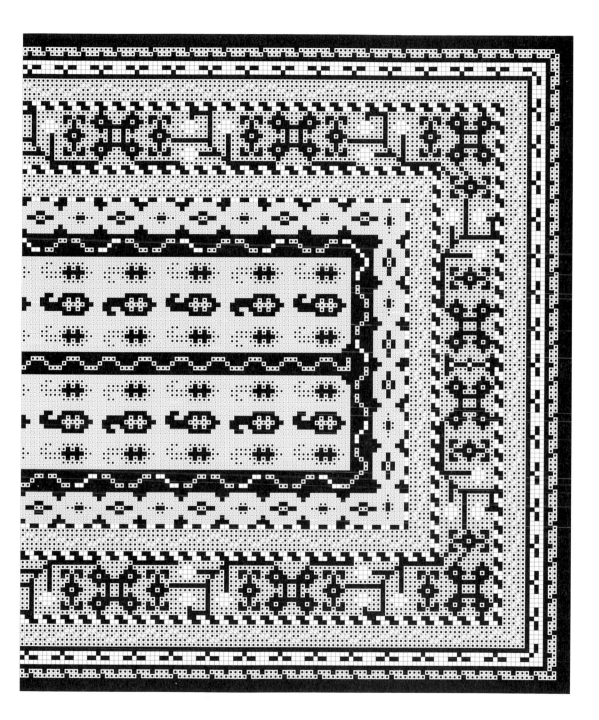

HAMADAN

The city of Hamadan is about 150 miles southwest of Tehran, on the site of the ancient biblical city of Ecbatana, where the tomb of Esther and Mordecai is located.

Hamadan is the seat of government for the province that has the same name and is also the trading center for the many villages that surround it. Although there may be some difference in the quality and design of the small rugs produced in the villages, the rugs are generally called Hamadan when they have been sold from that city.

The design for this rug is adapted from illustrations in *The Persian Carpet* by A. Cecil Edwards and *Oriental Rugs in Color* by Preben Liebetrau. The colors were adapted from Liebetrau's book, as the illustration in the Edwards book is in black and white. In both books, the background of the rug is described as a camel-hair brown, and the design as shades of red, blue, gold, and white, with a slight touch of green. The pole medallion is rather typical of the Hamadan district. The woven rug is approximately 54 × 83 inches.

There are several other characteristics of a Hamadan rug that help in identification. For example, the design is generally simpler than that of other Persian rugs. Also, the homespun yarn is heavier than that from other villages, and the pile is cut high. These heavy, hard-wearing rugs may lack the refinement of some other rugs, but they are a good value.

93 × 155 stitches
#18 canvas (18 per 2.5 cm)
5¼ × 8½ inches (13.5 × 21.8 cm)

Colors	Camel	Red	White	Brown	Green	Blue	Gold
Yarn #	442	840	445	440	690	570	752
Strands	8	12	12	6	10	12	4
Symbol	□	⊙	◩	⊡	⊠	■	⊡

KURDISTAN

The Persian Kurds occupy an area in northwestern Iran, extending from Hamadan to the borders of Turkey and Iraq. This area is very mountainous and inaccessible, and except for the tribes living in the less rugged eastern region, the inhabitants are nomadic or semi-nomadic.

In Kurdistan there are three types of rug weaves, which differ greatly from each other: the weave of the nomadic or settled tribes; the weave of the city of Bijar and its forty or more surrounding villages; and the Senneh weave found in the city of the same name.

The nomadic rugs are more rustic and unsophisticated than those made in either of the two cities. Those from the Bijar area are more densely tied with heavier material so that the finished rug has to be rolled instead of folded to prevent it from cracking. The Senneh rugs have more numerous and softer warp threads; both the warp and weft are cotton instead of wool. Because there are twice as many warp threads as usual, the weft must be thinner and the yarn spun finer. The knots are clipped more closely so that the design shows up more clearly. The end product is a thin, soft, flexible rug with a beautiful and exquisite sophisticated design.

The rug that inspired this design is in the McMullan Collection in the Metropolitan Museum of Art in New York City. The original rug is 48 × 62 inches.

More colors are used in this rug than in any other rug in the book. At first you may not see them, but if you look at the two borders, you will find them all. Even though some colors are used in very small quantities, they add a certain amount of verve to the finished rug.

159 × 218 stitches
#18 canvas (18 per 2.5 cm)
8⅞ × 12¼ inches (22.8 × 31.4 cm)

Colors	Dark Blue	Medium Blue	Light Blue	Ivory	Red	Green	Gold	Yellow	Coral
Yarn #	500	512	514	445	860	604	741	443	931
Strands	48	5	5	26	18	14	10	2	2
Symbol	■	⊡	⊠	☐	⊙	⊠	◺	⊡	⊞

SERABAND

In northwestern Iran, just west of Hamadan and east of Kermanshah, close to the lofty mountain Alvand, is where Seraband rugs are woven. There are several hundred villages in the area, all producing rugs of essentially the same design—the same simple pattern being used generation after generation.

A Seraband rug has a red, blue, or white field, which is filled with rows of *boteh* ("pine" or "leaf"), facing left and right in alternate rows. If the field is red, the boteh will be blue; if the field is blue, the boteh will be red; if the field is white, both colors will be used for the boteh.

In the rug that inspired this design, the white background of the main border is filled with elongated boteh of the same color as the field. This main border is about the same width as the combined width of the two adjacent borders, which are filled with undulating vines and rosettes. The outer border has the omnipresent trefoil motif, balanced by a sawtooth border that encloses the field. This description, found in Walter Hawley's book *Oriental Rugs, Antique and Modern*, guided me in designing this miniature.

The boteh featured in this rug is also found in other Persian rugs, such as in the Baluchi prayer rug on p. 99. In the West, we know this design from the Paisley shawls made in Scotland, where it was copied from the shawls of the Kashmiri, who in turn had taken it from the rugs of Persia. This boteh design really did get around.

179 × 253 stitches
#18 canvas (18 per 2.5 cm)
10 × 14³⁄₄ inches (25.6 × 37.8 cm)

Colors	Red	Blue	Gold	Green	Ivory
Yarn #	931	500	443	643	444
Strands	60	48	16	24	18
Symbol	●	■	◻	⊠	☐

SHIRAZ

A kilim is a flat rug with no pile, woven on a loom, with vertical warp threads and horizontal weft threads. To create the design in the rug, the weft threads do not extend from selvedge to selvedge, but rather they are woven back and forth around selected warp threads to form blocks of color. As a result, there's a slit in the fabric where two colors meet. For this reason, a straight perpendicular line cannot be more than a few weft threads deep, or the strength of the rug would be diminished by the long slit. If long vertical lines are part of a design, they must be slightly irregular, as they are in this rug.

A kilim is not as sturdy as a pile rug, because it doesn't have the hand-tied knots that reinforce the warp and weft. If a kilim is used as a rug, however, the custom of removing shoes when entering a domicile will ensure its relatively long life.

Kilims are produced in almost all the same areas where knotted rugs are made. They are made with little or no pattern when they need to be especially strong. Walter A. Hawley wrote that they are often used as pads under more expensive rugs and also in place of felt in covering tents.

This design is adapted from another illustration in *Rugs and Carpets* by Nathaniel Harris. If you're wondering why I have adapted so many designs from that book, it's because they are all so beautiful. This was also one of the first books about Oriental rugs I acquired. It was given to me in May, 1978, and in the fall of that year, I drew my first chart and made my first miniature rug.

139 × 280 stitches
#18 canvas (18 per 2.5 cm)
7³/₄ × 15¹/₂ inches (19.9 × 39.7 cm)

Colors	Black	Red	Orange	White	Blue	Green	Salmon	Brown	Dark Red
Yarn #	420	861	883	465	500	931	882	422	920
Strands	20	24	6	25	14	2	3	3	18
Symbol	■	●	◹	□	⊠	⊟	◺	⊓	◉

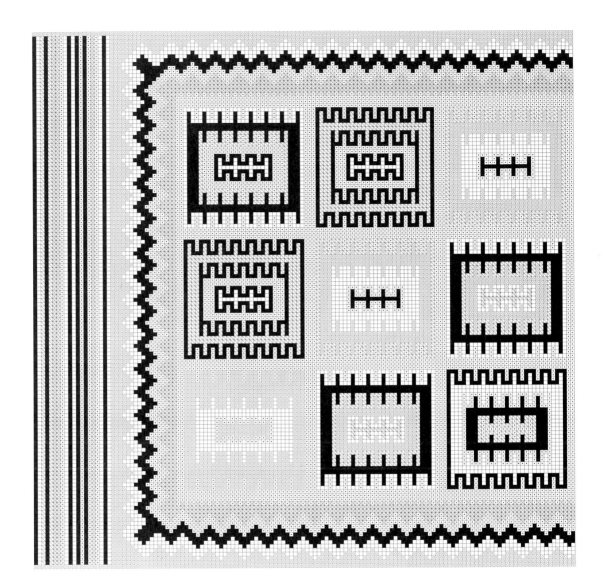

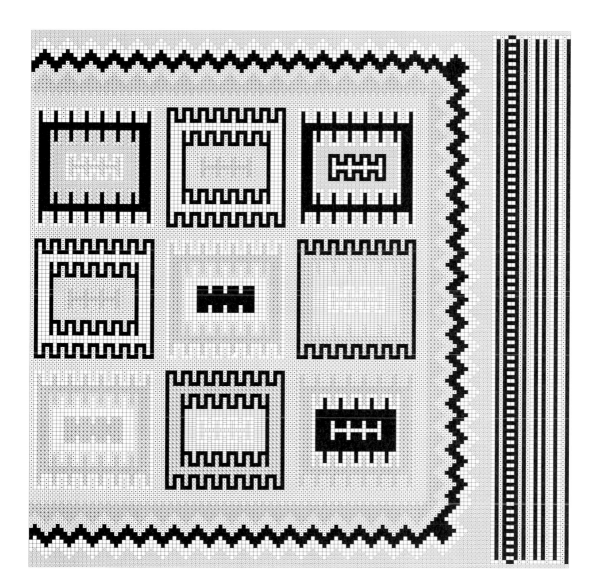

BIBLIOGRAPHY

Bennett, Ian. *Rugs & Carpets of the World*. Secaucus, New Jersey: The Wellfleet Press, 1988.

Bode, Wilhelm v., and Kuhnel, Ernst. *Antique Rugs from the Near East*. Ithaca, New York: Cornell University Press, 1984.

Cuadrado, John. "The Magic of Carpets." *Connoisseur*, December 1982.

Curatola, Giovanni. *Oriental Carpets*. New York: Simon & Schuster, 1981.

Dodds, Dennis R. *Oriental Rugs*. Richmond, Virginia: Virginia Museum of Fine Arts, 1985.

Edwards, A. Cecil. *The Persian Carpet*. London: Duckworth, 1975.

Gans-Ruedin, E. *Caucasian Carpets*. New York: Rizzoli International, 1986.

Harris, Nathaniel. *Rugs & Carpets of the Orient*. London: Hamlyn Publishing, 1977.

Hawley, Walter A. *Oriental Carpets, Antique & Modern*. New York: Dover Publications, 1970.

Holt, Rosa Belle. *Oriental & Occidental Rugs*. Garden City, New York: Garden City Publishing, 1937.

Jacobsen, Charles W. *Oriental Rugs*. Rutland, Vermont: Charles E. Tuttle, 1979.

Kerimov, Liatif, et al. *Rugs & Carpets from the Caucasus*. New York: Penquin Books, 1984.

Kybalova, Ludmila. *Carpets of the Orient*. London: Hamlyn Publishing, 1969.

Liebetrau, Preben. *Oriental Rugs in Color*. New York: Macmillan, 1963.

McMullan, Joseph V. *Islamic Carpets*. New York: Near Eastern Art Research Center, 1965.

Schurmann, Ulrich. *Oriental Carpets*. London: Octopus Books, 1979.

Thompson, Jon. *Oriental Carpets from Tents, Cottages, and Workshops of Asia*. New York: E.P. Dutton, 1988.

INDEX